AMERICA'S NUMBER ONE
OBNOXIOUS INDIVIDUAL SETS FORTH
A TOTALLY TASTELESS ARRAY OF HIS
MOST CHERISHED INSULTS!

THE PSYCHOLOGISTS UNANYMOUSLY
AGREE! JAMES HALLETT HAS DEFINITELY
SURPASSED THE ACCEPTABLE LEVELS OF
DECENCY IN WRITING HIS VERY OWN
BOOK OF THE INSULTS THAT HAVE MADE
HIS TONGUE ONE OF THE DEADLIEST
WEAPONS KNOWN TO MAN (OR WOMAN,
FOR THAT MATTER)! ARM YOURSELF
WITH A COMPLETE ARSENAL OF VERBAL
ASSAULT CERTAIN TO ENABLE YOU TO
RENDER YOUR VICTIMS HELPLESS.

TRULY TASTELESS
INSULTS

JAMES HALLETT IS AMERICA'S
NEWEST MASTER OF INSULT HUMOR.
HE APPEARS REGULARLY AT MANY
OF THE TOP NIGHT CLUBS ACROSS
AMERICA AND HAS RECENTLY
COMPLETED A TOUR OF EUROPE AND
AUSTRALIA.

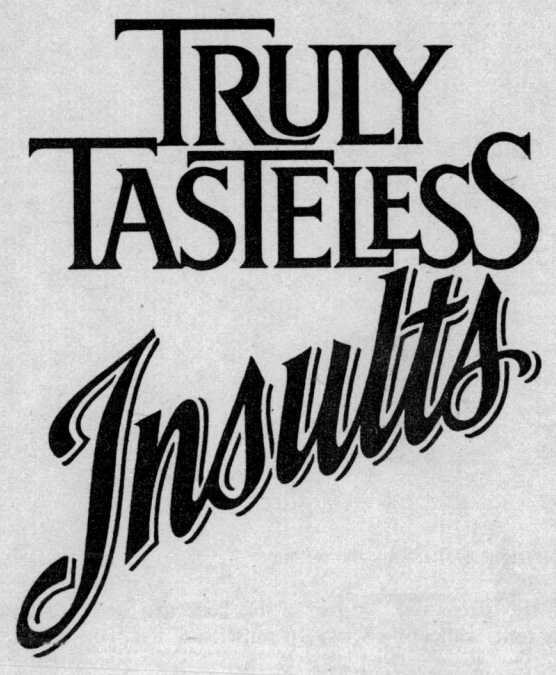

TRULY TASTELESS Insults

JAMES HALLETT

Copyright © 1988 by the author

All rights reserved. No part of this book may be reproduced in any form without the written permission of the publisher.

Reprinted by arrangement with the author

ISBN: 1-55547-229-X

Manufactured in the United States of America

DEDICATED TO MY MOM, THE ONE LADY I'D NEVER INSULT.

Boyfriend/Husband

Nice girlfriend—did you hire her for the night?

How did you get your wife down the aisle, did you throw a bone and yell "fetch?"

Do girls actually go out with you?

If you want to jerk off, I have a pair of tweezers you can borrow.

Your girlfriend likes chewing on bubble cum.

Who performed your wife's abortion, Captain Hook?

I heard you applied for a loan—from the sperm bank?

*

I can't seem to find my penis, can I look in your wife's mouth?

*

So, your girlfriend tells me you're a premature ejaculator.

*

Where'd you pick up your girlfriend, at the pound?

*

You say you're well-hung, how do you measure, by the pubic inch?

*

I didn't know your girlfriend worked at a whorehouse.

*

Your wife's like playing bridge—she's a good partner and has good hands.

That's funny, I heard you were hung like a chipmonk.

You said your wife had a craving for seafood, so I gave her crabs.

If I want to hear dumb stories about you, I'll listen to your wife.

Is that your ego in your pants or are you smuggling yams?

How would you like to have sex with a real man? (Woman): No thanks, I'll stick with fakes like you.

I'll bet you have ESP—Extremely Small Penis.

I'm curious, when your wife gets her period, how much money does she lose that week?

You're so cheap that when your wife wants to take a late-nite bubble bath, you make her eat beans for dinner.

*

That skank's your wife?!

*

The only difference between your daughter and garbage is that garbage gets picked up at least once a week.

*

That looks like a dick, only smaller.

*

When they told you to use your Dictaphone, you told them your penis was too small to dial the numbers.

*

Does your wife buy her cookbooks from the Humor or from the Horror section?

*

Is that your dick or a tattoo?

My guess is that you've never seen a pussy.

*

How's the slut and kids?

*

Do you always keep a pencil in your pants?

*

Know what I like about you? You make me look good.

*

You know what they say about guys with big thumbs. Big thumbs mean big assholes.

*

It's not size that matters, it's technique. Technique aside, though, penetration would be nice.

*

If you want my advice, pay me.

*

Isn't your other wife a blonde?

There's a word for guys like you and it starts with ka-ka!

*

I'll bet you haven't had sex in a long time.

*

I want you to eat me on my period.

*

You're pretty small for a man, aren't you?

*

That's your wife?

*

Are you related to George Custer?

*

You deserve a wife and kids.

*

Nice to meet you, Mr. Sharkbait, er . . . Smith.

**HOW DO YOU CLEAN YOUR NOSE?
ROTO-ROOTER?**

The difference between your wife and a bowling ball is you can only get three fingers in a bowling ball.

*

From where did you graduate—Pro-Folac Tech?

*

When you jerk off, your hands fall asleep.

*

I heard that you got a penis transplant and your hand rejected it.

*

Your wife tells me it now takes all night to do what you used to do all night.

*

Your girlfriend doesn't like pantyhose, she likes a rubber hose.

*

Yeah, I know, you're the guy with the small dick.

It must be hard going through life not being able to get it up.

*

What'd your wife do last week, entertain a stag convention?

*

People think you're the garbage man because of all the trash you take out.

Girlfriend/Wife

I like you. You just don't give a damn about how you look.

I love the way your boobs jump around when you dance.

I can see myself in the grease on your nose.

I'll ask for your opinion after I give it to you.

I've been looking for a woman like you—short, fat and dumb.

Have I called you "Varicose Face" today?

*

Where did you learn to cook blackened chicken?

*

I wish you were a little more anorexic, I'd jump your bones!

*

I'd like to get to know you better, do you accept major credit cards?

*

You're a classy girl, lower classy.

*

The older you get, the younger I feel.

*

If I had a mug like yours, I'd fill it with cheap beer, too.

*

Sure we've met. Tijuana, '78. Remember your friend the donkey?

Your cooking reminds me of you, foul and smelly!

*

Been using that salmon douche again, Dear?

*

I know about your blowjobs, you bend over and fart on someone's face.

*

The only reason you like wearing sleeveless dresses is because you like the feeling of the wind blowing through your hair.

*

The only difference between you and my dog is my dog doesn't wear tacky nail polish.

*

Those look like tits, only smaller!

*

You have one thing in common with a tampon—you're both stuck up cunts.

Your new fur coat matches your moustache.

You give great head-ache.

What perfume do you use—Le Douche Bag?

Does the word ugly mean anything to you?

Is one of your breasts larger or did Laurel and Hardy leave you their heads?

No, I wouldn't call you a dumb blonde, especially since your roots are black.

Nice body—for a gorilla.

You could use a new bra.

That's a nice dress, it hides your body.

Your husband told me he wants what you can't give him—proof the kids are his.

Did your doctor prescribe something for around-the-clock protection?

You're just like a chicken farmer, you both make a living out of raising cocks.

You're so stretched out, you can use your diaphragm as a trampoline.

When you put your bra on backwards, it still fits.

When you stopped talking for a minute, I was worried I had gone deaf!

You don't have a beaver—you have a skunk!

You remind me of a warm toilet seat—I wonder who was there just before me.

Do you bleach yourself?

You've got child-bearing lips.

You're the type of woman I like to put on a pedestal—tie a rope around your neck, and kick out the pedestal.

Before you put on your make-up, don't forget to shave.

Your husband told me you were bi-sexual; he also told me twice a year was not enough for him.

TRULY TASTELESS INSULTS 23

You wanted to become a hooker but you blew the job.

Tell me, does your latest girlfriend fuck all your friends, too?

Why are you limping, did you cut your toes shaving?

Your household must be a real circus, because you're a real clown.

I hear vice picks you up a lot.

You're a lot like stale beer, I get no head from either of you.

You've had so many facelifts that if you have one more they'll call you the bearded lady.

You stopped wearing a bra to draw the wrinkles out of your face.

You're such a whore, you bought a used car just to get screwed.

When you went fishing with a bunch of guys, all you came home with was a red snapper.

Where'd you get the necklace from, a vending machine?

I see you bought a new pair of shoes. What are they, open-toe bowling shoes?

You're such a snob even your period is French Provincial.

They won't let you go swimming because they can't get the smell out of the fish.

I'd rather fuck a bear trap—it's safer!

Who braided your underarms?

Sex

Your wife thinks that sex with you is such a chore she lets the maid do it.

Your girlfriend's idea of birth control is kicking you in the shins to make you limp.

You and your wife are sexually compatible—you both have headaches at ten.

So what happened when you put your dick in her hand, she said "No thanks, I don't smoke cigarettes!"

Q: Why did the wife kill the fisherman?
A: He caught too many hairy clams.

What mouthwash do you use—piss water?

*

You look like you mistakenly used Ben-Gay to jerk off with.

*

I didn't say you were a pick-up, I said you probably ride like one.

*

How about some cheesecake, Baby?! No, a mincemeat pie sounds good enough.

*

You're as exciting as they come. Unfortunately, they come better.

*

If I had a choice between fucking your pussy or fucking your face, I'd keep it to myself.

*

You look like you could spare a rubber.

Would you like a mayonaise sandwich?

You remind me of something gooey.

Do your dates shoot themselves in the foot just so they can leave early?

You remind me of Grizzly Adams—the guy who fucked bears.

Your mother told me she almost didn't have you— she kept using her head.

Your relationships go very deep—seven inches.

Oh! You actually slept with a woman?

Your father's a midget. What did your mother do, suck the height from him?

Your little boy told me that when he caught you having sex, you explained to him that you were making him a baby brother. He also told me the baby won't be arriving because he saw the milk man eating it yesterday.

Did anyone ever tell you you have small hands and feet?

What'd you wear to console the widow—a black rubber?

Don't worry about other guys getting your girlfriend pregnant—she only gives blowjobs.

When you ask your wife "Has the paperboy come yet?" does she reply "No, honey, he's just breathing hard?"

After you screw your wife, do you always want a camel?

You come from such a hick town the hooker is a virgin.

The reason you like big tits and small pussies is because you've got a big mouth and a small dick.

You never fail to find a date with a complexion problem.

All right, all right, hold yer herpies!

Do you belong to Sex Without Partners?

You couldn't score if you played on a nymphomaniac girls' volleyball team.

What came all over you?

*

Don't be nervous, it's just the whole world watching.

*

I don't want to make love with you, I'm in too good a mood.

*

Sex with you! I'd rather chug a mug of broken glass.

*

Have you tried laying off the S & M food parties?

*

I'll bet you fucked just about everybody.

*

You're faking this whole thing.

*

Do you masterbate while you drive?

Man: You're the perfect lover, my wife's gonna kill me!
Woman: You're the perfect lover, my husband's gonna kill you!

*

You bring out the animal in me.
It's a good thing I like mice.

*

Where have you been all my life?
In bed with your wife.

*

I wouldn't have sex with you if you were the last man on earth—why stop with only one to go?

*

How would you like ten inches?
Ten inches? I didn't know you had nine friends.

*

Can I help you?

You're like porn without sex.

You're a jack of all trades, mostly off!

Intelligence

I can insult your intelligence any time it warrants my doing so.

Did you get that at Budget Brains?

If you only had a brain.

Please go on, I wasn't listening anyway.

Let me get this straight, you are an idiot, and I'm talking to you, is that right?

You have an ingrown brain.

YOUR GIRLFRIEND'S SO UGLY, THE LAW REQUIRES SHE WEAR A PAPER BAG OVER HER HEAD.

You have a defective understanding.

＊

That's the tenth time you've been wrong today.

＊

Thanks for falling asleep, I was worried you'd say something.

＊

First day with the new brain?

＊

And they say you're an idiot!

＊

I'd give you a piece of my mind, but it might overburden you.

＊

You've got a clear head. I can see right through it.

＊

You're a mental virgin.

How can we use your ignorance to my advantage?

*

I love listening to your voice, it's so stupid!

*

What do you do for a living, write insult books?

*

Where'd you learn to lie with such a straight face, the KGB?

*

Who hired you, the janitor?

*

Is than an experimental expression?

*

You're a good joke, now tell one.

*

Yes, I know ridicule, I get it for talking to you.

Thanks for your opinion, I'll forget it always.

*

You climb the corporate ladder, I'll catch the executive lift.

*

Excuse me, I think I just stepped in your personality.

*

One more complaint and you're fired.

*

What makes you think you know what you're talking about?

*

I miss your razor sharp wit, will it ever arrive?

*

How did you learn to kiss your own ass like that?

*

That's the best pitch I've heard all day—too bad I don't care.

What about a little pick-me-up? How about a little put-you-down?

*

Why don't you give up and let the rest of us relax?

*

Have you considered employment as a talk-show host, or do they require a minimum intelligence?

*

This is what happens when they fuck with DNA.

*

Please don't say any more, your mind can't handle the strain.

*

I hate it when you think you know something.

*

Do you need help, or do you want to fuck it up?

*

You are the only real fool I know.

Greed got you where you are today, nowhere.

With my brawn and your brain, we'll at least lift something.

I'd give you the benefit of the doubt, but you've already messed that up.

You're so stupid, I'll bet it hurts.

What's a good way to shut you up?

I love it when you wimper.

When you make chocolate chip cookies, it takes you nine hours to peel the M&M's.

The only thing you play on your walkman is a tape "left, right, left, right, left . . ."

Is it true you sold your waterskis because you couldn't find a lake on a hill?

The last time you were so stoned and lit your joint, your dick hurt for a month.

At the movies you kept buying a new ticket because the guy at the door kept tearing yours in half.

I heard about your new business venture, self-service massage parlors.

I'm sure whatever you had to say wasn't important.

I'd ask your opinion if I thought it was important.

If you were a race car driver you'd have to ask directions at the Indy 500.

You're so stupid that when you pull into a gas station and see a sign "clean restrooms" you scrub the toilets.

I'm afraid to cut off your fingers fearing you'll lose the ability to count to ten.

Oh—you must be stupid.

Why are you so happy? Did you just find out your AM radio worked in the afternoon?

It's strange—you look intelligent.

That's a plan, if you want to fail.

You have the brain capacity of cartoons.

YOU'RE SO FAT, YOU DON'T TAKE BATHS, YOU TAKE CAR WASHES.

They gave you a degree?

At the table, you stand up with a piece of bread just to make a toast.

You'd try to move your house just to get rid of the slack in the clothesline.

When the forecast says one foot of snow, you only wear one boot.

I tell ya—you make the kid from *Deliverance* look like an intellectual.

Does your mother still buy your clothes?

You say you're intelligent—when does it start?

Did you buy your brains at K-Mart?

You loaded suppositories into a gun and asked your friend to blow your brains out.

If I didn't know you, I'd swear you were a retard.

You're so stupid that when you see a sign at the movies "under 17 not admitted" you invite 18 friends.

On the camping trip, when you were told to pitch your tent, you threw it at a bat.

The only thing you ever invented was a solar powered flashlight.

I'd like to pick your brain, but I see you've already picked it clean.

Thanks for your opinion, but no thanks.

*

You're the last in a long line of idiots.

*

May I haul you over the coals?

*

Your lips move when you think.

*

Thanks for calling, I needed a break from my everyday wonderful life.

*

Ah, the TV generation.

*

You must have an enormous brain cramped into that small head of yours.

*

If ignorance was bliss, you'd be having an orgasm.

If shit were brains, you'd be a genius.

*

Nine times out of ten, you're wrong.

*

Your ears listened while your mind took a hike.

General

Your family tree has root rot, and it bears stupid fruit.

*

Your brain is in your pants.

*

I'd like you more if I saw you less.

*

So, tell me . . . what's it really like at the bottom?

*

Ahh! A meal fit for a peasant!

*

Ahh! A meal fit for a pigeon!

Have I died and gone to Disneyland?

∗

Are you struggling to overcome this insanity thing?

∗

Life got you down? Good!

∗

Have you filed for Ayatolla status?

∗

Your mother is bald.

∗

You've been using that garlic and onion mouthwash again.

∗

You should be ashamed of something.

∗

You have tuna breath.

YOU WERE SUCH AN UGLY BABY, FOR THE FIRST SIX MONTHS THEY DIAPERED YOUR FACE.

You are an insignificant pusbag.

We were just laughing about you.

Why worry, you're going to fail anyway.

Is that a hat, or are you drying your underwear?

You're an international embarrassment.

You'll love spinsterhood.

Hey, Dolt! Have another donut.

You're unable to function in this society, have you tried Borneo?

You've developed a new social disease, crampies.
I get them when I listen to you.

*

You smell like steaming hog guts.

*

Your face and a goat udder.

*

You are a dum hinger.

*

Have you got lice?

*

You fuck goats!!

*

Are you worm enough?

*

Were your parents influenced by Hitler?

54 *I. Q. Anonymous*

You remind me of a loser, is that you (Bill, Joe, etc.)?!

Why do you think they call you a dope?

Your tailor must really have a sense of humor.

You might get more votes if you stopped tongue kissing babies.

You have a way with words . . . a bad way.

On a scale from one to ten, you suck.

Have your parents been introduced?

Your parents should have done more acid in the sixties.

Has anyone ever called you a shithead?

*

You provide adequate nightmare fodder.

*

You're an endless supply of revulsion.

*

I'm mentally slapping you.

*

You new C.D. player is one of the cheapest made.

*

You're kin to slugs.

*

You are a visual stank.

*

You're a gas, butt gas!

Do you still wet the bed?

*

You're an international disgrace.

*

You are the strained vegetable in a world of fresh produce.

*

The devil knows your name, and it's Norman.

*

You're a unique individual, a one of a kind asshole.

*

You look in the bowl before you flush.

*

Have you sought professional help for your petty problems?

*

If you want my advice, pay me.

You're in social solitary (confinement).

Better close your mouth, you're losing precious bullshit.

I bet you have plenty of regrets.

If you had it to do all over again, would you still make a wreck of your life?

Let's see. Your skin is pink, you're all puckered up, shit comes out of your mouth, you must be an asshole!

What sign are you, fork in road?

What made you decide not to run in the human race?

Does your mom put you on hold?

*

Your wallpaper is the color of pus.

*

Will you be drinking more tonight, sir? If not, we'll invite everyone back.

*

What happened to your car? It's so cheap.

*

You're an intense individual with an inner cleft lip.

*

I know, I know, you're not a gynecologist, but you play one on T.V.

*

You park like you look, crooked.

*

Would you like a tissue, or are you going to let it just HANG THERE!?!

You smell like rotten eggs.

*

Mmm! Is this gas station coffee?

*

You're Attila the waitress, right?

*

You are a known carcinogen.

*

You're desperate for retention.

*

Have you always been a little scum-sucker.

*

I keep seeing your face wherever I go, it makes me sick.

*

Einstein was right. In this case, my reaction to you is regurgitation.

THEY CALL YOU THE TRASHMAN BECAUSE OF ALL THE GARBAGE YOU TAKE OUT.

TRULY TASTELESS INSULTS   61

Who peeled you off the stool?

The IRS just called. They want to use you as an example.

I never met a man I didn't like, until now.

Do your grandkids still call you wrinkles?

Those are your feet?!

No dessert, thanks, you can't put a sugar coating on slime.

Were you born this way or did your parents do something stupid?

Do I get another cup of coffee or shall I call a Contra?

I wouldn't be caught dead with you on my mind.

*

This guy eats charity for breakfast.

*

You're a tourist in your own home town.

*

Eat shit and die.

*

Eat dye and shit blue.

*

You'll be infamous for half an hour.

*

You remind me of someone important. You couldn't be him/her!

*

You smell as bad as you look.

I missed what they said about you, it was something about being an asshole.

Don't look at me, I'm not your mother.

What would you like for your birthday, a toothbrush or a bar of soap?

Is that flypaper, or a tie?

You're not serious about having children?!

Did a cat crap in your pockets?

I admire you . . . very little.

You're the best with less.

Who let you in?

May I milk your venom for scientific purposes?

You insipid shit!

You're in the hype of fashion.

Your breath is as sweet as clover, after the cow has eaten it.

I don't hate you half as much as everyone else.

Isn't there a flu named after you?

Have you learned much from humans?

Don't be so hard on yourself, let me do it!

*

Is that your fairy dog mother?

*

Why do all my friends leave when you show up?

*

You're built like a shit brick house.

*

Your mother shaves her butt.

*

You couldn't get the time of day from a telephone operator.

*

You don't have any qualities, let alone likeable ones.

*

I'd love to be at your funeral.

You'd make a good politician/lawyer.

✱

You must be a burden on your kids.

✱

Do you claim a nationality, or shall we call you mammal?

✱

How'd you get a driver's license, inheritance?

✱

You've almost got it all, good looks, money, prestige. If you only had a friend.

✱

Please have a seat . . . er, downwind.

✱

Do the nose and feet come with the family name?

✱

Are you on the fingernail diet?

WITH EARS LIKE THAT, DID YOU EVER CONSIDER FLYING?

I've got money riding on you; I just don't care any more.

*

Is this your famous mouse rump soup?

*

Do you save your gallstones?

*

If you leave me anything in your will, please, don't let it be that suit!

*

I think you pooped in your pants.

*

In this modern age it's nice to meet a backward fool like you.

*

You smell like a pig with the runs.

*

Where did you learn how to drive, Taiwan?

Where did you learn how to drive, in a demolition derby?

Would you like a dog to go with those fleas?

I understand the first thing your grandfather did just after your parents were married was lower the shotgun.

How'd you break your finger—somebody punch you in the nose?

Sniff! My guess is you've never missed an important call because you were in the tub.

What'd your father do? Marry a buffalo?

Did you steal your clothes from a Salvation Army bin?

Nice clothes—circus back in town?

*

Cute haircut—what did the barber use? A pencil sharpener?

*

You've got worse breath than my dentist.

*

My guess is you don't believe in baths.

*

What are you looking at, Dicknose?

*

Your mother's so fat you have to use side view mirrors to see around her.

*

Nice pants—was there a flood?

*

You are real nice for a jerk.

Look at you, your life's a wreck.

You're so cheap, when your girlfriend wanted to frost her hair, you stuck her head in the freezer.

When you asked the protologist for a second opinion, he stuck another finger up your ass.

Your grandpa's so mental, he was throwing stale bread to the planes at the airport.

Your mom's such an idiot she planted Cheerios in her garden because she thought they were donut seeds.

Your mother used to dunk her tits in milk to breast feed you.

What's that smell on you—vomit?

Your barber must have a real sense of humor.

*

You're really becoming a class act—is that an olive I see in your beer?

*

You forgot what you had to say? How about goodbye?

*

You've been shit on so many times they call you John.

*

You've been stepped on so many times they call you Matt.

*

I wish more people like you would stand up and all leave the room together.

*

This is my friend the midnight sailor.

You look like you just jogged home from your vasectomy.

*

You look good with a couple of drinks in you. You look better with a bottle of booze in me.

*

What are you looking at, Moosehead?

*

Your apartment's very nice. I saw it in Better Homes and Garbage.

*

You've got class—all low.

*

What are you going to send for your resume—blank paper?

*

Have you ever had a normal haircut?

You're too insulting for mere words.

You have a problem with going to the bathroom in the morning—you piss at eight, shit at nine, and wake at ten.

Your dog is a lot like your cold sore, it won't heal.

Your mother still hangs your sheets out to dry.

I hear you like to play hide and seek. Tell me—who'd come looking for you?

You come from such a hick town the 7/11 is called 2/5.

You come from such a hick town that during the fashion show they hold up a J.C. Penney catalogue and point.

Why worry, you'll probably die anyway.

*

When your grandpa goes out to eat at someplace fancy he orders Alpo under glass.

*

I heard the supermarket doubled its sales on pet food when they offered your grandma a senior citizen discount.

*

Is that a tie-dye or did someone spit paint on you?

*

Anyone tell you that you talk like Lou Ferrigno?

*

You couldn't get a job at McDonald's.

*

You wear brown suits so the shit stains don't show.

Your father's a plastic surgeon who specializes in fixing tupperware.

When your mother told you to put on a new pair of underwear each day, by the end of the week you couldn't put your pants on.

The only difference between you and a bucket of shit is the bucket!

When you were a baby you were breast-fed by your father.

Ever think of using deodorant?

You must have no hemorrhoids because you're such a perfect asshole.

I found out the magic words your mom said to your dad to make him marry her—"I'll sue you for child support."

So you're what happens when relatives marry?

You're so dumb, when they told you you had to take a drug test, you thought it meant to see how many drugs you can put in your body at one time.

How can you respect yourself?

My wife tells me you just got out of prison.

*

You have very small hands and feet, they say that means . . .

I heard you were kidnapped as a child but your parents said keep the body.

When you were kidnapped as a child and they sent one of your fingers back to your parents, your father said he wanted more proof.

Don't you feel embarrassed wearing bell-bottom suits?

*

Your mother wears Army boots.

*

You're so stupid . . . when your wife asked you to change your baby son, you came back an hour later with a baby girl.

*

I heard they turned you down for the janitor's job because you didn't know how the wastebaskets worked.

*

Anyone tell you you smell like fish bait?

*

I hear your pet rock ran away.

*

How'd your tongue get black, did someone pour whiskey on a freshly tarred road?

Your grandma almost starved to death because an alley cat mugged her on the way home.

✱

Are you a deadhead, or a colorful slob?

✱

You should be more defacing.

✱

You are a credit to your card.

✱

Do you need an environmental impact report before you bathe?

✱

I've got to admit, I'm a better man than you.

✱

Do dogs mistake you for friends?

✱

You should be addicted to something.

TRULY TASTELESS INSULTS

And the weak shall inherit the earth.

I'm sure we'll benefit from your ignorance.

We needed a new bullshitter around here. Thanks for showing up.

You look like shit.

Cancer of the personality; bummer.

Ethnic

You remind me of a fresh road kill.

I wouldn't call you sleazy, but you are.

Nice shoes, did you mug a bowler?

I can't take my eyes off of you, and you can't take your eyes off my wallet.

Is that a tooth missing, or are there flies in your mouth?

Did you ever think it's time for Ike Turner?

*

You didn't evolve from apes, you evolved from skunks.

*

How do you live with the agony?

*

You're an urbane failure.

*

There's a booger on your shirt.

*

You look like someone just threw a shit pie in your face.

*

Are you black, or dipped in shit?

*

I don't think we've met. I've never been in prison.

Don't you play the frugal horn in the Jewish Symphony?

*

You're a new minority.

*

I bet the reason you have a doormat inside your house is to make sure the street doesn't get dirty.

*

When you take a bath, I bet you leave an oil slick.

*

You live in such a bad neighborhood that the stork doesn't deliver babies—the drug dealer does.

*

You probably got your wife pregnant by exchanging underwear.

*

You came from such a low high school, I'll bet your class rings were beer pull tabs.

You know—they invented the wheelbarrow so you could learn to walk on your hind legs.

Chico, I heard you're suffering from insomnia—you keep waking up every ten days.

You're a nigger, right?

You're a spic, right?

Where do you shop, Bowling for Clothes?

You know a lot for a guy who was never adopted.

You're tough. I'll bet you could press 100 pounds with your lips.

So this is your famous rat stew?

You're such a Jew that you probably have no qualms about abortion, because you feel life doesn't begin until medical school.

What's your idea of an Italian ice, a frozen cesspool?

What's your family's idea of a formal dinner, all the men come to the table with their flies zipped up?

Your kid's so black and stupid, the only noise he thinks a pig makes is a siren.

You're half Irish and half Italian—do you mash potatoes with your feet?

Chico, the reason you haven't won the Nobel Prize yet is because the committee won't come to New York to read your literary work off the sides of trains.

If you're so smart, Tyrone, what's the name of the guy fucking your momma last week.

All the Nazis had to do to round your grandparents up was roll pennies down the street.

Hey, Jerome, in your new Cadillac they didn't install seatbelts, they just put Velcro on the ceiling.

When you want a cold lunch, all you do is stick ice cubes up your nose.

Were you born that way or did you get burnt in a fire?

Does this sound familiar, "Look up, face forward, face left?"

Why so down, Tyrone? Can't afford a taxi to the welfare office?

*

Tyrone, there's three things you can't get from me—a black eye, a fat lip, or a job.

*

Hey, Leroy, the last time you had a rabbit dinner, two of your brothers had to look both directions to watch for cars.

*

When you fly home to Puerto Rico this year, are you going to fly their national airline, "Air Pollution?"

*

Burn any crosses lately?

*

Tyrone, the reason you can't become a ventriloquist is very few dummies will work for a darkie.

CLASSIC INSULT: YOUR MOTHER WEARS ARMY BOOTS.

You're so poor your front lawn is a dandelion in a flower pot.

*

Yes, Chico, I heard about your new car pool—you and a bunch of friends pushing a car to the unemployment office.

*

Hey, Goldberg, I just saw your new porno movie, 20 minutes of begging, 5 minutes of sex, and 55 minutes of guilt.

*

Tyrone, I hear your father's organs didn't go to waste after all, an orangutan got his heart, a baboon got his heart and kidneys, and a gorilla got his eyes.

*

Your favorite summer sport is waterskiing through carwashes.

If you were a burglar you'd be caught for wearing glow in the dark bowling shoes.

Hey, Geraldine, does your new black cherry lipstick come with its own paint roller?

Guido, the reason you haven't discovered any new stars yet is because you refuse to work nights.

Your family doesn't know what an ashtray looks like without a motel logo on it.

You're such a racist you'd fuck a polar bear because it was white.

Why won't you get a blowjob, Leroy? Afraid you'll lose your welfare checks?

You must be Mexican! Your refried brains gave you away.

*

Guido, your girlfriend's so hairy, she shaved herself so she wouldn't be picked up by the fuzz.

*

Your mother's like a bowling ball—black, three holes, and gets rolled in the gutters.

*

What kind of cigars do you smoke—Non Producto?

*

You smell so bad even blind people can hate you.

*

What kind of spaghetti do you eat—Regresso?

Hey, Dong, what's your favorite cookbook—101 ways to wok a dog?

Chico, you're so dumb that you spray paint graffiti on chain link fences.

Hey, Tyrone, I notice you don't ski, is it too hard to hold a pole in one hand and a radio in the other?

Leroy! The reason your father died in Vietnam is because when the squad leader yelled "get down" your father got up and danced.

There's barf on your shoes, you better eat it before one of your family does.

Did you say something, or are you practicing your Bronx cheer?

You definitely have an advantage over the impoverished.

You drool very well.

Fat

You eat a lot of food—don't you?

*

You're so fat that every time you lie down three Marines plant a flag on you.

*

You fat mass of flesh.

*

Have another jelly roll, stick it to your belly roll.

*

She eats like a bird—vultures aren't very pretty during mealtime, either.

Is your hair thinning out, or is your head getting fatter?

You're all hips and thighs. How do you find room for fat?

Is that fat, or a body hat?

You are an island surrounded by a sea of sweat.

Did you swallow a pot belly stove?

He was a tall fat kid who never needed to grow up.

Oh, hoarding blubber again?

Are you going to share your birthday cake this year?

*

I've never seen anyone work out with pudding before (pump'n pudding).

*

That's quite a bon bon collection you have there.

*

You're so fat you can only play seek.

*

When you moved, the supermarket went out of business.

*

You're so fat that when I want to fuck you, the only hole I can find is your navel.

*

Next to you, Santa Claus looks thin.

All I can make out of you is a bologna sandwich.

*

What'd you do—swallow a beach ball?

*

What do you wipe your ass with—a parachute?

*

I didn't know guys could get pregnant.

*

Your wife has to bat her eyelashes by hand.

*

When you get a blowjob you have to take the girl's word for it.

*

What do you do to clean your wife—take her through the car wash?

*

You could never drown—fat floats.

The Russians track you by satellite.

They just assigned you your own zip code.

How many meals to you eat in one sitting?

Did you swallow Dom DeLouise whole?

Still pregnant after all these years?

I see you've taken up imaginary weight-lifting.

I'll have the filet mignon and a side of beef for my fat friend.

I'm glad you're not a nudist!

WHAT GRAVEYARD DID THEY DIG YOU UP FROM?

You must be a pretty fast swimmer to have never been harpooned.

*

Did you suck the filling out of those jelly rolls?

*

You are a blob, but that's just a figure of speech.

*

You are what you eat, and you eat a lot!

*

You're so fat you have to oil your butt to pull on your pants.

*

Where did you get that Goodyear T-shirt?

Gay

Are you the guy with the velvet undies?

*

I'll bet you thought no one noticed?

*

You look like a girl.

*

You run like a girl.

*

You laugh like a girl.

*

You blow guys like a girl.

Did you make the change in Sweden?

*

Is that yogurt in your eye?

*

Is there a cure for people like you?

*

You're a lesbian in a man's body.

*

You sold your soul for a stinky hole.

*

You're flirting with death and he's not gay.

*

There's ham-jam on the corners of your mouth.

*

Your ass just died.

Have you got anal swelling?

You're such a fag that you grew that moustache to hide the stretch marks.

I bet you have AIDS—Adios infected dick sucker.

What's your idea of a meat locker—a male chastity belt?

I heard you got fired from the sperm bank—drinking on the job!

When you're through drinking will you zip up my fly?

I heard your date last night was a real winner—big brown eyes, big firm tits, big hairy dick.

I just heard you're gay—is that why you always come in the back door?

*

I bet you get turned on by the full moon.

*

All you get when you cross you with a gay Eskimo is a snow blower that doesn't work.

*

Your designer jeans have a zipper in the rear.

*

How'd you break your finger—what'd you do, sit down?

*

You are a woosie and so's yer dad.

*

You are what you eat, you must eat a lot of fruit.

I'd shake your hand, but you might not let go.

*

How'd you become gay—did a friend suck you into it?

*

Your test came back from the dentist—you have V.D.

*

It must have been quite a blow to discover you were gay.

*

Your boot camp was so gay they couldn't separate the men from the boys.

*

Was that fart your homosexual mating call?

*

How come you've got a sign on your dick saying "No chicks accepted?"

You'd call a row of urinals a smorgasbord.

*

Tell me—do you miss prison?

*

So you're gay, huh? What's that mean—Got AIDS Yet?

*

In the Air Force you requested to be tailgunner.

*

If you were a politician you'd probably kiss men's hands and shake babies.

*

I never knew a gay Jew before. What are you—a He-blew?

*

I don't understand why you're gay—did your teacher assign you fairy tales?

Your boyfriend probably refers to your hemorrhoids as speed bumps.

You want me to go over to your place so you can show me your etchings—no thanks, I'll wait for the etchings to stop.

Do you have an accent or is your mouth full of sperm?

Sure I'd like to have sex with you, as soon as I've acquired AIDS.

Does it hurt when you sit?

You were Redd Foxx's gay lover.

What's that white coating on your tongue?

Has your mind gone flat, or did you just blow a re-tread?

Who asked you—dick face?

You've got a firm grip on your priority.

I've heard you can be a pain in the ass, I'm not letting you near mine.

You're a fag who likes women.

Ugly

You have a kind face, the kind that melts cheese.

*

Your hair is falling out in blotches.

*

Your wife is so ugly, Idi Amin wouldn't eat her.

*

Are you growing a trunk?

*

He makes most fish look attractive.

*

I didn't say you had big ears, you must have imagined it from way over there.

The insults aren't pretty, but neither are you.

*

Did a jeep rape your face?

*

If I had a face like yours, I'd go into punk rock.

*

Are you okay, or do you always keep your lips in your shirt pocket?

*

Gaping frogs look better than you.

*

Your face should be on Mt. Rushmore, it's big and full of cracks.

*

I like your freshly sick pallor.

You've got lovely teeth, would you mind taking them out so I can get a better look?

*

Looks like someone forgot to take off your feed bag.

*

Your eyes are like pearls, your face an oyster.

*

You're a cross between Margaret Thatcher and Willard Scott, but looks aren't everything.

*

You look like that monster, you know the one, old what's his name . . .

*

I'm writing a book about your life, it's called *Acne*.

*

There's a bugger on your eye.

Zit farmer, eh? Sheesh! Looks like it's time for harvest.

*

Is that your baby, or did an elephant shit in your blanket?

*

Beauty is only skin deep. Maybe you should peel off another layer?

*

Is that a birthmark or are you growing an outer liver?

*

I was just wondering, have you been bald all your life?

*

I thought you were dead!!

*

Is that your nose or a blow up globe?

It looks great on you . . . what is it?

*

Zoo let you loose, eh?

*

You have nice skin, is it imported?

*

You have nice skin, is it an antique?

*

Let's void this relationship before you can get more ugly.

*

Who pushed your face in? Will it pop out unexpectedly?

*

Did you have your nose enlarged?

*

I like your convertible forehead.

Have you gotten an accurate count on those chins?

Ugly is definitely hereditary, at least in your family.

Who drilled out those nostrils?

There's mold in your eyebrows.

You should've insured your face earlier—you could have used the coverage.

That's your nose?!

Your mother must be truly sorry.

You sure you never boxed?

With ears like yours, did you ever consider flying?

The girls at your college are so ugly their dorms are called pig sties.

Did somebody give you a fat lip—or were you born that way?

That's one hell of a nose—how do you clean it? Roto-Rooter?

It's amazing what they can do with plastic surgery these days.

You're proof the missing link exists.

I heard the hospital made your parents keep you.

YOU'RE SO STUPID, YOU SPRAY GRAFITTI ON CHAIN LINK FENCES.

You were such an ugly baby the gypsies returned you.

You remind me of a sick joke.

Boy, vice grips really do some damage, wouldn't forceps have been safer?

Do seagulls search you out or do you catch whitewash for a living?

Anyone ever tell you that you have fish lips?

You remind me of John Carradine when you look at me like that.

If looks could kill, I guess I'd be dead.

If looks could kill, you'd be miserable.

*

With a face like yours, thank God my memory's bad.

*

Were you born that way or were you kissed by a wrecking ball?

*

You look like a model—for abstract art.

*

You're so ugly, the nurse enema'd your face.

*

With teeth like yours, why do you bother to brush?

*

You're so big and hairy they wouldn't let you leave the zoo.

You're so ugly that when you were born the doctor slapped your mother.

*

Who does your hair—Don King?

*

Nice ears, can you pick up cable T.V.?

*

Why are you trying to save face when it's as ugly as yours?

*

It's a shame you couldn't find a good toupee.

*

Your mom puts a paper bag over your head before she kisses you good night.

*

Then she puts one over her head in case yours falls off!

I have something here that might get your teeth clean—a box of sandpaper.

What graveyard did they dig you up from?

You look like Michael Spinks.

You're so disgusting, germs won't go near you.

Did you ever think there's a reason I don't call you?

Ever think of taking up drowning?

You're the reason they introduced air pollution acts.

You look like you just fell off a truck.

Oh, I didn't know the sideshow was back in town.

The way you look, when's the funeral?

You look like my favorite movie star—Godzilla!

You were such an ugly baby, for the first six months your parents let the zoo take care of you.

I hear you were second in a beauty contest, Ernest Borgnine came in first.

Your feet are so big, you could squash watermelons into wine.

You've never looked in a mirror, have you?

*

Congratulations—I'm sure the baby'll be as ugly as you.

*

There's shit on your teeth.

*

You've got a point there, right on your bald spot.

*

You've got a face only a mother would slap.

*

Better look up an embalmer.

*

You have big dumb ears.